Weather in Fall

by Mari Schuh

Bullfrog Books

Ideas for Parents and Teachers

Bullfrog Books let children practice reading informational text at the earliest reading levels. Repetition, familiar words, and photo labels support early readers.

Before Reading:

- Discuss the cover photo. What does it tell them?
- Look at the picture glossary together. Read and discuss the words.

Read the Book

- "Walk" through the book and look at the photos. Let the child ask questions. Point out the photo labels.
- Read the book to the child, or have him or her read independently.

After Reading

- Prompt the child to think more. Ask: What is the weather like in fall where you live? What do you wear outside in fall?

The author dedicates this book to Katie Krizek of Racine, Wisconsin.

Bullfrog Books are published by Jump!
5357 Penn Avenue South
Minneapolis, MN 55419
www.jumplibrary.com

Library of Congress Cataloging-in-Publication Data
Schuh, Mari C., 1975-
  Weather in fall / by Mari Schuh.
      p. cm. — (Bullfrog books. What happens in fall?)
  Summary: "What do people do in the changing weather of fall? Color photos and easy-to-read text tell kids all about how people adapt to the season of changing weather"—Provided by publisher.
  Includes bibliographical references and index.
  ISBN 978-1-62031-061-8 (hardcover : alk. paper) —
ISBN 978-1-62496-079-6 (ebook)
  1. Weather—Juvenile literature. 2. Autumn—Juvenile literature. I. Title.
  QC981.3.S344 2014
  551.6—dc23
                                                        2013001953

Series Editor: Rebecca Glaser
Series Designer: Ellen Huber
Book Designer: Heather Dreisbach
Photo Researcher: Heather Dreisbach

Photo Credits:
Alamy, 7; Corbis, 12–13, 23tl; Dreamstime, 5, 10, 22; Shutterstock, cover, 1, 3b, 4, 6, 11, 14, 15, 16–17, 18, 19, 20, 22 insets, 23bl, 23tr, 23br, 24; Superstock, 9, 21

Printed in the United States of America at Corporate Graphics in North Mankato, Minnesota.
5-2013 / PO 1003
10 9 8 7 6 5 4 3 2 1

Table of Contents

Fall Weather

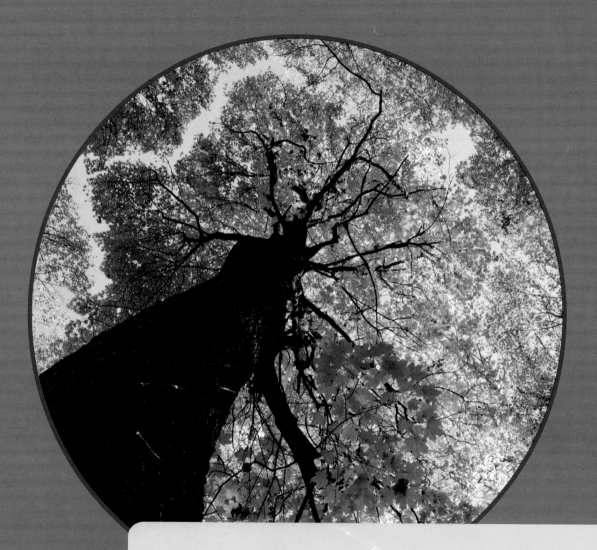

The warm summer is over.

Now fall is here.

5

Fall is a season of change.
In fall, the weather is cooler.

The temperature drops.

In fall, the air is cool and crisp.

Noah wears a jacket to stay warm.

Selma wears a sweater.

Some fall days are
warm like summer.

Yay! Today is sunny.

Jake plays outside.

11

Some fall days are chilly like winter.

Brr! Kay can see her breath.

13

Some fall days are rainy.

Splash!

Jill jumps in a puddle.

Some fall days are windy.
Whoosh! Ethan sees leaves
blow in the wind.

frost ·······▶

Fall weather gets colder
and colder.

Frost covers the ground.

Plants freeze.

Fall is almost over.

Soon, winter will come.

What do you do in fall?

How Warm Is It?

snow

frost

32°F/0°C
water freezes

rain

Picture Glossary

breath
The air taken
in and out of a
person's mouth.

puddle
A small pool
of rainwater.

frost
A thin layer of
tiny pieces of ice.

temperature
How hot or cold
it is outside.

Index

To Learn More

Learning more is as easy as 1, 2, 3.

1) Go to www.factsurfer.com

2) Enter "weatherinfall" into the search box.

3) Click the "Surf" button to see a list of websites.

With factsurfer.com, finding more information is just a click away.